Motivational Words
From Your Favorite Gym Teacher

*Written for Athletes, Coaches, Adults, Young Adults,
Anybody needing a lift in life*

By George Bertos

authorHOUSE®

AuthorHouse™
1663 Liberty Drive
Bloomington, IN 47403
www.authorhouse.com
Phone: 1-800-839-8640

First published by AuthorHouse 12/15/2010

ISBN: 978-1-4520-9932-3 (sc)
ISBN: 978-1-4520-9933-0 (dj)
ISBN: 978-1-4520-9934-7 (e)

Library of Congress Control Number: 2010917546

Printed in the United States of America

This book is printed on acid-free paper.

Certain stock imagery © *Thinkstock.*

158
Bertos, George
Motivational Words From Your
Favorite Gym Teacher

Table of Contents

The following pages were written with love and heart. They are intended to motivate and inspire anyone needing a lift in life. These thoughts are meant to touch people as they experience a variety of life situations. They have various meanings for different people.

If I took a pen name it would be the "Running Writer". Most days during the summer I jog three to five miles around Park Lake in Rockaway. As I jog, these motivational poems come into my head. I began to write them down. The next thing I knew I'm writing a book. This book took me two summers, and over 200 miles of jogging to complete.

If your life is made a little more positive through these words, then I have achieved my goal.

Dedication:

I would like to thank the Lord for these words that I put into print...

My wife, children, family, and friends for the courage and confidence to publish these words...

My sister in law who has guided me through the publishing process. I never could have accomplished this without her knowledge and great attention to detail.

My students, past and present, for believing in me and motivating me to motivate others...

Thank you from the bottom of my heart!

Chapter One

Messages To My Graduates

Believe in yourself
Take on tomorrow's challenges
Give it your best shot
And you can always walk away
With your head held high

If you try your hardest,
And give one hundred percent
Whether you win, or
Whether you lose
You will have won…

A man should not be judged
by his accomplishments,
But by his efforts to accomplish

When all is said and done,
don't ask yourself,
Was I the best?
Ask yourself
Was I the best I could be?

Why is man obsessed with sport?
All the emotions of life are involved in sport
Sport is a mirror image of life
If you understand life, you will enjoy life
If you understand sport, you will enjoy sport

The question is not, did you win or did you lose?
The question is, did you play to your fullest potential?
If the answer is yes, then you must be satisfied

Life is not about what you did,
It's about what you are about to do...

Tomorrow will be whatever the Lord makes it
Tomorrow will be a most beautiful day

Always try your best
Put all your faith in God
And good things will happen

How hard would you play today
If you knew you couldn't play tomorrow

Attempt everything in life
With your best effort
And a great passion
And you will be happy

Keep the Lord in your heart
Then, play with all your heart

God gave us all a Gift
If the gift he gave you is to be athletic,
then it is up to you to use that gift to it's fullest potential
You'll never know what level your gift is unless
you always work and try your hardest
Only then will you be satisfied and fully realize your gift

The most precious thing on earth is life
There is no dollar sign large enough to be put on the value of life
Perhaps people can't see the forest for the trees
Perhaps people are looking for the pot of
gold at the end of the rainbow,
But are missing the rainbow
Time is very fast on this earth
Take time out, stop...look...listen...
Enjoy the beauty of the earth,
Enjoy Life...

Good sportsmanship and best effort
If you take these two things with you in life
The only failure you will have in your life
Will be the days you don't take a chance
Be of good courage
And take that chance

Give It Your All

All the yesterdays are gone
No one knows how many tomorrows lie ahead
But as for today – Give It Your All
Success is nothing more than a person's will to
relentlessly work toward a goal
The will to persevere in the eyes of doubt
Remain focused on your dreams and visions
Give It Your All
Don't be consumed with first or last
God has given us each a talent
Find your talent and have fun with it
Give It Your All
Be it in friendship, in love, in work, in school,
In athletics, in life----to be truly happy
Give It Your All

Lord…
Give our children the strength to be the best they can be
Give us, their parents, the strength to accept whatever they become

Chapter Two

Religious Inspiration

If thou canst believe, all things are possible
to him that believeth.

* St. Mark 9:23

*From The Holy Bible, King James Version

*St. Luke 7:23	Blessed is he, whosoever shall not be offended in me.
St. John 20:29	Blessed are they that have not seen, and yet have believed.
Romans 5:3,4	Tribulation worketh patience; and patience, experience; and experience, hope.
Deuteronomy 31:6	Be strong and of a good courage, fear not, nor be afraid of them: for the Lord thy God, he it is that doth go with thee; he will not fail thee, nor forsake thee.
St. Mark 11:24	What things soever ye desire, when ye pray believe that ye receive them, and ye shall have them.
Romans 10:11	For the scripture saith, whosoever believeth on him shall not be ashamed.
10:12	For there is no difference between the Jew and the Greek: for the same Lord over all is rich unto all that call upon him.
10:13	For whosoever shall call upon the name of the Lord shall be saved.

Religious words that have inspired me.

* From the Holy Bible, King James Version

Chapter Three

The Athlete

"I firmly believe that any man's finest hour, the greatest fulfillment of all that he holds dear, is that moment when he has worked his heart out in a good cause, and lies exhausted on the field of battle---victorious"

Vince Lombardi

"Gentlemen, we are going to relentlessly chase perfection knowing full well we will not catch it, because nothing is perfect. But, we are going to relentlessly chase it, because in the process we will catch excellence."

Vince Lombardi

One of my favorite motivational speakers of all time.

Why Do You Run
(Why Daddy Why)

I Run

    Because in this world it is important to practice what you preach

I Run

    Because the ancient Greeks believed a healthy
    body and a healthy mind go hand in hand

I Run

    Because it conditions my body and frees my mind

I Run

    For the health of it. An exercise in perseverance.
    Going nowhere, but escaping to everywhere

I Run

    So I might be in this world a little longer

I Run

    For you my children
    I run for you

This truly is why I run.

Stand Up My Friend

We work extra hard every day
Waiting for our chance to play

We may not have the size
We may not have the weight
But under our jersey
You can see it palpitate

Look at the drive, sense the desire
It is what keeps our hearts on fire

Stay patient as you wait your turn
Don't throw away all you have learned

The time has come to play this game
Stand up my friend and grab some fame

Growing up, I was always the smallest kid in the class.

Training Again

The wet cold weather has gone out to sea
The sun shines down eighty two or three

Your lungs are filled with the warm fresh air
You begin to train like no one would dare

Your goals are set, the sky is the limit
You pace yourself each day to the minute

Dripping in sweat, your shirt getting wetter
Pushing your legs to make yourself better

It's great to be back, training with no resistance
Follow your heart, one day you'll make a difference

Spring, 2010.

I'm Back

I was gone for a while
With two bad knees
My hamstrings they used
To repair both of these
They said I was done
I'll never be back
Watch me my friend
You've never seen Jac
I work every day
I push till I drop
Some day down the road
I'll be the cream of the crop
My mom and my dad
They make me believe
The day will come soon
When I will achieve
My stick in my hand
I'm back on the turf
Make up for lost time
One goal will be first
Now I am back
Enjoying every minute
Taking nothing for granted
My dream I can win it

For my daughter upon returning to her sport after two ACL surgeries.

Running In The Rain

The skies have opened
Everybody cleared out
The rains came down
They all started to shout

I run all alone
The wind in my face
No one can stop me
I keep the same pace

Don't let the obstacles
Get in your way
Run from your heart
With each passing day

The sun has returned
Along with it comes the heat
People stay away
But I refuse to be beat

My work is soon over
I built up my muscle
The countless hours put in
Allow me to hustle

A beautiful summer day to run.

Courage

Courage is something
    Found deep inside
Under your shirt
    But no place to hide

It comes out when you need it
    That's for sure
Able to do great things
    In love and at war

The time has come
    Your time is now
Dig deep if you must
    Your opponent will bow

Never relinquish
    The strength you were given
Never be afraid
    Step up and start kickin'

Only you know what's inside.

I Love The Heat

It's mind over matter
You learn to play through it
A definite advantage
If you let yourself do it

You'll need plenty of water
Train at a steady pace
Turn it into a game
And enjoy the race

You must put in the time
The work must get done
The heat as your friend
In your mind become one

Few people left out there
They've succumbed to the heat
If your mind can stay strong
You will never be beat

A sip of some water
And one extra mile
You do this for you
With nothing but a smile

When people say you're crazy
No need to hide
Turn up the heat
And enjoy the ride

Softball and Little League baseball games played in 102°.

Always A Champion

When your journey begins
    There will always be doubters
    Always be negative people
    Always be naysayers
    Always be people laughing
If you can see your way through this
    You Are A Champion

There will always be roadblocks
    Always be crossroads
    Always be an easier road to follow
    Always be a shortcut
If you can fight your way through this
    You Are A Champion

Stick to it when people tell you to quit
    Dig deeper when the well runs dry
    Stay focused on your dreams
    When distractions mount up
Put forth your best effort no matter what the score
    You Are A Champion

If you can persevere through all the people
    All the obstacles
    All the temptations
Everything that stood in your way along your journey
    You Will Always Be A Champion

About the 1999 football team…
Turn of the century.

Stand Tall

Nobody's perfect
Look deep inside
Into your heart
Nothing to hide

The world of athletics
Is a wonderful place
You train on your own
Stay ahead of the pace

How far will you go
That nobody knows
Sacrifices made
Through highs and lows

When times get tough
You must dig down deep
The work that you did
You must trust your feet

In the end you will find
If you gave it your all
The effort was worth it
And now you stand tall

Never Surrender

You may get pushed around
    You may get knocked down
Never give in
    No Surrender
The battle may be long
    At times you must be strong
Never give in
    No Surrender
The spirit lies within
    That pushes you to win
Never give up
    No Surrender
Uncounted hours put in
    To lose would be a sin
Never give up
    No Surrender
To fight with all your might
    That is why you came tonight
Never give up
    No Surrender
Leave it all on the field of play
    No matter what the others say
Never give up
    No Surrender
Stand true to your goals
    When you're hardest hit
When your back's against the wall
    You must never quit
Never give up
    No, Never Surrender

Fitness For Life

I preach every day
    Go at your own pace
Each one of us different
    Slow, no disgrace

The trick is to start
    Get up off your butt
Pick up a friend
    Climb out of that rut

Time waits for no one
    You must find a reason
Overweight, out of shape
    Or maybe you're wheezin'

No more excuses
    No reasons why not
Your friends and your family
    Say get up off that cot

So much to offer
    So much to give
Walk for the health of it
    The longer you'll live

The choice is yours
    Not tough to decide
So what will it be
    Get up or go hide

Yearly class trip to Lewis Morris Park.

TEAM

You're only as strong
    As your weakest link
A team united
    Must never blink

Some may be fast
    Some may be strong
Must find a spot
    Where we all belong

Some are our leaders
    They live to excel
They pull from the front
    And push us as well

We give our best effort
    One hundred per cent
We'll never be broken
    At times may be bent

There is no I
    There is no me
We'll all stand as one
    One we will be

Raise Your Game

There's more to being a great athlete
    Than just being the best player
Check your ego at the door
    Must ignore the nay sayer

You may possess the greatest strength
    You may be the fastest runner
Without the proper attitude
    You may always be a mudder

Must be willing to sacrifice
    To give one hundred and ten
Willing to help your teammates
    Be better in the end

Must be a good role model
    For future generations
Kids able to look up to you
    Envision their destination

Must be able to accept criticism
    To raise your game's level
Close your mouth, open your ears
    And watch the coaches marvel

In your head, you must slow down the game
    While moving at top speed
You'll see the game more clearly now
    Playing with great ease

I've given you some tips today
    How badly do you want it
Now leave it all on the field of play
    And surely you will get it

Chapter Four

Life

"Some men see things as they are and ask why, I dream things that never were and say, why not."

Robert F. Kennedy

"Each time a man stands up for an ideal... he sends forth a tiny ripple of hope."

Robert F. Kennedy

The Game Of Life

This game, like all games,
will be whatever you make it
If you give your best effort
you will have fun and success
If you walk aimlessly through the game,
you will neither have fun nor success

Achieve

To climb the highest mountain
You can achieve it
To accomplish your heart's greatest desires
You can achieve it
Any time people say, it'll never be done
You can achieve it
Believe in yourself, Believe in the Lord
No chains on earth can ever hold back
One's will to achieve
If you want it badly enough
You can achieve it

Make A Difference

Nobody knows how long you will be here
Make A Difference
One kind, positive word to a person who is down
May change their life forever
Make A Difference
God has given you the strength and the courage
Be not afraid
Make A Difference
Nobody knows the strength that lies within you
Know thyself
Make A Difference
You are but one person
Yet one person can change the world
Make A Difference
One thing for certain
You will never be here again
Wait no longer
Make A Difference

I believe each of us can make a difference.

Live

One thing we all know
One day it will end
Live for today
All people your friend

Be of kind heart
Be gentle with all
When your time is up
The Good Lord will call

So much we could do
So much we could give
For you to decide
How you will live

It's not the money you have
Or the things you display
It's the blessings you get
Every night when you pray

Be not afraid
Of your heart's desire
He will always be with you
When you walk through the fire

Persevere Forever

When the going gets tough
Lift up your chin
Don't quit my friend
You must never give in

You may get knocked down
You may get kicked around
Pick yourself up
Without even a sound

At times the climb may seem
All uphill
That's the time to fight
With all your will

Life's battles will be a challenge
A challenge you should treasure
Push with all your might
Persevere forever

Heart

You may be strong
You may be smart
To reach your dreams
You gotta have heart

The road will be long
The road will be rough
I know you can do it
You gotta be tough

You will climb over mountains
You will cross through rivers
Never stop fighting
Until you deliver

At times you'll be tired
At times you'll be weak
Stick to the fight
You're nearing the peak

It will all be worth it
Looking back at the start
You made it my friend
You did it with heart

My Wife

When you take your vows, you take them for life
One woman, one woman, one woman, one wife
For rich and for poor, for better, for worse
God as your witness, may you never thirst
With disagreements and different points of view
Stand by her side and you will see it through
The good times, the celebrations, together you will share
The memories everlasting, with more than just a tear
Always a compromise, you can't always have your way
Love her for who she is, love her from day to day
Communication is a key, you must always talk things out
Talk to her softly, there is no need to shout
Be true and be honest, she is your best friend
May you live long and be happy, together till the end

Happily married for thirty years.

If I'm Not Here To Say Goodbye

You were my angels sent from heaven above.
The joy you brought to my life could never be
equaled. I thank you for all your love.

I pray every night that you have the strength
and the courage to do the work of the Lord.

To be kind, to be thoughtful, to be caring,
and help others aboard.

Put all your faith and trust in his rhymes.
I promise you, my children, for all of His work that
you do, He will give back to you one hundred times.

May your lives be long and healthy. May you
enjoy the beauty of every day. Be thankful for all the
little things God has given you today.

I am so proud of each of you for who you are,
and who you have become. I am the luckiest man on
this earth to have been sent three beautiful angels
from above.

I love you more than words could ever describe.
May love always flourish throughout your lives.

I will always be with you…A place in your heart…
Must say goodbye, for now we must part…

To my children.

Old Glory

Living in America
    Free as a bird
Must be responsible
    Live by your word

Let freedom ring
    From coast to coast
Watch each other's back
    From the 9/11 ghost

Our flag is flying high
    Blowing in the breeze
We'll defend it forever
    Our enemies will freeze

Be thankful for what we have
    We must give to the world
May our kindness be returned
    Every day our flag is unfurled

Don't look behind
    You cannot change the past
Focus on today
    May Old Glory Everlast

Written on the 4th of July, 2010.

Crossroads

In your life
    You will hear many voices
Some say come this way, others, go that way
    In the end you make the final choices

Follow your heart's desire
    No matter what they say
Live like there's no tomorrow
    Enjoy each and every day

In times when you are down
    Take one step at a time
The Lord is always with you
    Look upward to the sky

Every choice you make
    Will surely change your life
Sooner or later
    You may even take a wife

Be not afraid
    At times to take a chance
Believe in yourself
    You can make it to the dance

So when the time comes
    To make that decision
Keep the faith my friend
    Live life with great vision

A note to my Godson.

Keep The Faith

Once in a lifetime
> You'll have that lucky day

When all things are good
> No matter what they say

Some days it's a long climb
> You can make it to the end

Rest if you must
> Never give up my friend

We all have highs and lows
> We all get knocked down

Stand strong in your beliefs
> Keep your feet firm on the ground

Tomorrow shows great promise
> You can see the light ahead

You must keep pushing forward
> Live by what you said

Keep faith in what you have
> Your convictions should be strong

Let no distractions turn you
> Be successful and live long

So important to always keep the faith.

Life For The Taking

Enjoy every second of each and every day
Hope you can find time to get out and play

In a heartbeat your life can change forever
You must work hard to keep things together

Yesterday is over, we cannot bring it back
Find the love in your heart to forgive, and forget that

Everything's against you, oh so it seems
Turn to your church, your friends, hold on to your dreams

Good times will return, a betting man would say
Give it an honest effort, live for today

Easy, nobody said life would be, but life is for the taking,
To share with you and me

Character

It takes a lifetime to build
Someone strong in their ways
Can lose it in a second
One time, for all their days

Trust built through honesty
The more people join this race
Leadership by example
The world a better place

There's so much out there today
Influencing our plate
Must do what's right
Please, please, don't hesitate

Be well rounded and respected
That's what you're aiming for
Follow these few words
It will open many doors

When you sit across that table
You may not pass the test
But, one thing for sure
You always tried your best

You can hold your head up high
In spite of outward pressure
You live your life with truth
That only you can measure

Take A Chance

Sometimes in your life
    You must take a chance
Roll the dice hard
    Give it a glance

When opportunity knocks
    You must open the door
Good things await you
    Not afraid to take more

The risk may seem high
    The reward you'll never know
Unless you take a shot
    And let your emotions go

You go through life once
    Sometimes you'll get burned
Persevere and push forward
    Much wiser from what you've learned

When the time comes
    Unsure of what to do
Have faith and have courage
    The Lord looks over you

My version of "Imagine"

Imagine a world
    Filled with kindness and love
Nothing to fear
    But that from above

Imagine a country
    Where people are ready
Searching for peace
    To make the world steady

Imagine all nations
    Joining our plight
Freedom for all
    No one to fight

Imagine the power
    One voice can project
The right to speak freely
    Choose what you net

Imagine this your goal
    Whatever it takes
The world is made better
    By one man's fate

Could you imagine?

My Way

People think I'm crazy
    For teaching in Catholic school
No benefits, no pension
    They say I'm a fool

There's more than meets the eye
    It's not about the money
How about teaching kids with love
    And make each new day sunny

The games they love to play
    I teach them to believe
If you always try your hardest
    Some day you will achieve

To accept winning and be humble
    To lose is no disgrace
Keep pushing forward
    You must enjoy the race

One day they will grow up
    Their foundation should be strong
The Lord is their Shepherd
    Live happy and live long

St. Cecilia's, 1991 - present
St. Pius X, 2005 - present

The Journey

The day you were born
    That's where it all begins
Blazing your own trail
    Where no one else has been

The road may be long
    Many turns along the way
Over mountains, through forests
    New battles each day

You choose the path
    The challenges await
To enjoy each new moment
    The ride you must partake

Enjoy each precious day
    As if it were your last
Leave no regrets behind you
    When thinking of the past

It's never too late
    To change your direction
Be brave and have courage
    At every intersection

Wherever your road leads
    Helping people along the way
Sharing love and kindness
    Making brighter each new day

Encouragement

Before you could walk
    Before you could speak
Somebody pushed you
    Toward the top of the peak

Your Mom, Your Dad,
    Your Teacher, Your Priest,
Always behind you
    Feeding the beast

From riding a bike
    To driving a car
They made you believe
    You could go very far

You find fuel for your fire
    In many unknown ways
Each one of us different
    Till the end of our days

You never would have made it
    You've become who you are
From those few simple words
    Destined to go far

How fast they grow up.

Butterfly

The beauty of a butterfly
    Most people never see
The flutter of her wings
    Happy to be free

No two are alike
    Their features are unique
Enjoy their days of freedom
    While climbing to the peak

They always can sense trouble
    From the day that they were born
Searching for protection
    From the distant storm

Although they keep their distance
    In the trees above
Sometimes they fly before us
    Sharing their sweet love

The beauty of a butterfly
    Much like you and me
Trying to survive this planet
    From sea to shining sea

The most colorful butterfly fluttered across my path.

The Roller Coaster Of Life

The economy is slow
    Your debts are high
You lost your job
    You can barely get by

From generation to generation
    The world keeps changing
Hold your head up high
    It's time for rearranging

On the roller coaster of life
    We all go up and down
Keep an even keel
    Feet firmly on the ground

Never know how close you are
    No one knows how big the hill
At this point you mustn't quit
    Let drive and desire guide your will

As long as you remember
    Morning follows every night
You can conquer any challenge
    With good attitude and fight

To so many friends out of work, hang in there.

Walk A Mile

Walk one little mile
    To free your mind
Solving life's problems
    Leave them all behind

With the wind at your back
    It's easy to fly
With all odds against you
    There's no need to sigh

Don't allow the stress
    To bring you down
Nor the pressure brought on
    By some big mouth clown

As you cut through the course
    Hold tight to your ways
Good things await you
    All the rest of your days

Be not afraid
    Your will must be tough
Rise to the challenge
    From dawn to dusk

Walk one little mile
    That gave you your start
Now all others follow
    You lead with your heart

Homeless

Here you are, homeless today
    The bank, they took your house away

Fishing by the water's sod
    Still have your family, friends, and God

You drop your head as you begin to doubt
    Feel like quitting and want to shout

At these times when you're down and out
    Keep the faith, you musn't pout

No one knows what lies ahead
    Keep pushing forward, forward I said

You will make it through this day
    Rest if you must, sit and pray

The sun will shine on you tomorrow
    Leave behind the past, it's sorrow

Back on your feet, stand tall and show it
    Be strong, help others, your reward you'll know it

My homeless friend at Yankee Stadium.

Be Thankful For What We Have

As I begin my warm-up stretching by the bench at the lake, a young girl being pushed in her wheelchair by an elderly man approaches the bench. The old man sits on the bench to rest. The girl stutters ten times to get out each word.

Be thankful for what we have.

A woman with a stick in her hand, being led around the lake's path by a seeing eye dog and a trainer.

Be thankful for what we have.

A homeless man pulling his red wagon with all his belongings down toward the lake with a fishing pole in his hand.

Be thankful for what we have.

After I complete my jog, my cool down stretching is by another bench. There is a memorial plate on this bench of a boy who unexpectedly died when he was just seventeen years old.

Be thankful for what we have.

We have been given so much. Yet people always find something to complain about. Each and every day of your life try to do one kind thing for somebody, anybody, without being asked to. We can make this world a better place, one person at a time.

Be thankful for what we have...

Summer 2010

The Human Spirit

The fast and rushing waters
    With them the mud
Your house, it may be washed away
    But you'll survive the flood

A class five hurricane
    With great wind and great rain
May take all in its path
    But you'll be back on your feet again

A death in the family
    May break your heart
Though in the end
    We all must depart

The earth may quake
    Your life shattered
Pick up the pieces
    You've only been battered

The flames of a fire
    May engulf your house
The hoses, the firemen
    Will give it a douse

A disease in the family
    May consume your life
But the human spirit
    Will never give up the fight

Kill The Beast

Teal ribbons on the trees
　　Now what does it mean
National Ovarian Cancer Awareness
　　To make aware you and me

It reminds me of all cancers
　　People battle every day
Scientists searching for a cure
　　To rid this disease some way

This enemy has no eyes
　　It has no need to see
Black or white, young or old
　　It can attack you or me

Some we can prevent
　　Some we can delay
We must never give up the fight
　　Till we're cancer free one day

We must all work together
　　To kill this massive beast
Future generations will be thankful,
　　And live with great relief

September 2010

Children Of The World

If you lead them, they will follow
    So young, they know not sorrow
If you teach with love and kindness
    They'll grow up with prejudice blindness

Put a smile on your face
    They copy everything you do
Be fair and be honest
    They love to mimic you

Like it or not
    They grow up in a flash
Stand strong as a parent
    So their future may last

Say no to drugs and alcohol
    You must always stay ahead
Their friends may persuade them
    To places that you dread

Put the Lord in their heart
    That they may always know forgiveness
To get up when they fall
    Back on the road, with great strength, and wellness

Chapter Five

Thoughts
From My Daughter

Why Do We Play This Game

Why do we play a sport so unique
Why do we work till our bodies are weak

Why do we report to the track every day
Why do we come in August to play

Why do we run until our lungs are tight
Why do we eat and sleep hockey from morning to night

Is it for your parents who come to every game
Is it for your teammates who are cheering on your name

Is it for your coach, your number one fan
Is it for your friends or some special man

Do you play for the feeling of sweat down your face
Do you play for the intensity of an ongoing race

Do you play for the lessons learned from defeat
Do you play for the memories with the friends that we meet

Do you play for the glory when you finally score
Do you play for the feeling of being at war

We all play for one reason, I know that we do
Everyone on this team is thinking the same as you

Everyone's reason should all be the same
We're in this together for love of the game

Field Hockey

Courtney Bertos

57

More Than Dad

A brother, a cousin, a neighbor, a friend
Taking on so many roles, always a hand to lend

He is a husband to the love of his life
Enthusiastic and supportive this man and wife

The father of two daughters and a son
Whom he's taught to work hard while having fun

A role model, a motivator, a teacher
A follower of faith, an inspiring leader

The power of his words reaches out to us all
Teaching us to dust ourselves off whenever we fall

He finds the positive in every situation
He gives life and energy to every occasion

Stand tall, persevere, never say quit
All the encouragement has helped us each a bit

He practices all the things that he preaches
Little lessons along the way to all that he teaches

Believe in yourselves as he believes in you
With a little bit of faith, there's so much we can do

With motivational words or simply by his actions
He's helped so many people, if only by a fraction

I thank him for everything he's pushed me to do
Continue to inspire, the world's a little brighter because of you.

Thanks Dad!!

Courtney Bertos

Chapter Six

Final Thoughts

The Running Writer

Never set out to be a writer
   Gym is my game, could I get any higher
Words came out as I began to jog
   Wrote them down in my little log

No idea what to write
   Enjoy my run, wait with delight
Out of the blue, well what do you know
   Another title and away we go

Sometimes I forget the words
   Take another lap, write another verse
Thank you Lord for giving me the strength
   To run, and write this book with length

For each person I inspire
   A kinder world will transpire
My time on this earth will end one day
   But my words will live forever, lighting the way

Notes

Notes

Notes

Notes

Notes

Notes

Notes

Notes

Notes

Notes

Notes

Notes

Notes

Notes

Notes

Notes

Notes

Notes

Notes

Notes

Notes

Notes

Notes

Notes

Notes

Notes

Notes

Notes

Notes

Notes

Notes

Notes

Notes

Notes

Notes

Notes

Notes

Manufactured By: RR Donnelley
                      Breinigsville, PA USA
                      January, 2011